Bruce County

Georgian Bay

Lake Huron

Wiarton

Bruce County

Georgian Bay

Lake Huron

Wiarton

GROUNDHOG WILLIE'S SHADOW

written by
Barbara Birenbaum

A Story Within A Story© is two stories in one about the same theme, each uniquely different. They appear side-by-side on each page, to be enjoyed separately or together as one.

PEARTREE®

Published by
PEARTREE®
P O Box 14533
Clearwater, Florida 33766-4533
USA

Copyright© 2001

ISBN: 0935343-741

Printed in the United States of America
   10 9 8 7 6 5 4 3 2 1

Books by Barbara Birenbaum
The Gooblins' Night
Light After Light
Lady Liberty's Light
The Hidden Shadow
The Lost Side of the Dreydl
Candle Talk
The Lighthouse Christmas
The Olympic Glow

CIP Data
Birenbaum, Barbara

   Groundhog Willie's Shadow
      p.cm.
   Includes bibliographical references (p.)
   Summary: The story of Groundhog Willie of Wiarton, Ontario, CANADA, parallels story of first Groundhog Day of Canada and groundhogs in general.
   I. Groundhog Day - Juvenile Literature. I. Title.
GT4995.G76B57   2000   00-062426
394.261—dc21

Other Story's Within A Story©
Amazing Bald Eaglet

Dedicated to my husband for his enthusiastic support.

Dedicated to the memory of Willie of Wiarton, Ontario, the official Groundhog of Canada that made his final prediction the last year of the millennium. The tradition continues with Wee Willie of Wiarton.

Contents

Introduction

A Story . . .

This is the true story of how a very special groundhog became the official prognosticator and weather seer of Canada. From the very beginning, it became apparent that he would carry a message with greater insight than those around him ever realized. How his talents developed takes a lifetime to understand as he became known to the world as Groundhog Willie of Wiarton. It begins with the legend of the first Groundhog Day of Canada.

Within a Story

The origin of the first Groundhog Day of Canada gives deeper insight into the significance of this very special event. The locale of its beginning encompasses the home of Groundhog Willie. His unique appearance distinguishes him from other groundhogs, and those that predict the weather in the United States. It's up to the reader to decide what message is heard by which groundhog, where . . . All in the fun of Groundhog Day.

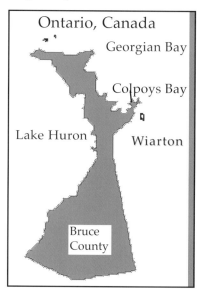

THE FIRST GROUNDHOG DAY

The story of Klionda, the Mohawk Indian, and Nawgeentuck, the Groundhog is known as the true story of the first Groundhog Day of Canada. By all indications, the weather was not easy to predict years ago. As the legend unfolds . . .

The fierce breath of the North God blew its song of hate as Klionda headed toward the Strange Land under the Polar Star. His limbs ached with fatigue for he had traveled for more moons than his fingers could count. The pale winter sun shone dimly through the snow-flecked sky and the great woods were still and silent except for the snap of frost against the hardwoods.

Many centuries ago, the Mohawks, one of the six Iroquois Indian tribes, settled by the Lake of Two Mountains Reserve near Oka, Quebec and the Gibson Reserve on Georgian Bay in Ontario. The first Groundhog Day of Canada evolved from the legendary encounter of Klionda, the Mohawk Indian and Nawgeentuck, the groundhog.

Other Iroquois, or Northeast Indian tribes were the Seneca, Oneida, Tuscarora, Cayuga, and Onandaga. Their land encompassed provinces of Canada - Nova Scotia, New Brunswick and Prince Edward Island, plus parts of Quebec and Ontario and a tiny part of Manitoba. The area extended from the Atlantic to the Mississippi River.

As Klionda trekked on, he recalled the familiar Valley of the Big River he had left long ago, and the longhouses of his tribe and those of the friendly Seneca, Oneida and Tuscarora Indians. He wondered if he would ever see the land of his fathers again. He thought of the Great Spirit, who was all seeing, and wondered why the great famine had come to the land.

Klionda thought of the valley he left behind, then the great hills and rivers of the beaver, and the Great Place of the Falling Waters, from where he could see a great, long bay.

The Iroquois thought of their combined territory as one large longhouse with the Seneca Indians, known as Door-Keepers, guarding the western entrance and the Mohawk Indians guarding the eastern entrance of their longhouses.

The Longhouse faith was founded by the Indian, Handsome Lake, in 1799. It incorporated traditional Indian tenets that existed many centuries before settlers came to the New World. It emphasized good deeds, silent prayer, and the belief in one god known as the Great Spirit. The Indian followers of this belief were farmers and corn planters. Their places of worship, like their homes, were longhouses.

As stark shadows of winter twilight became sharply etched on the rocky bluffs of the mighty bay, he made camp beneath the boughs of a fir tree, and he sensed the still forests and stone cliffs, frozen bays and lakes - and silence!

Klionda knew his strength was failing, and he would soon drift into a sleep from which there was no awakening. If he chewed the venison sinews from his snowshoes, he could gather strength, but to what purpose? With his snowshoes gone, he would be powerless to go further. As his mind drifted back to memories of the Valley and his beloved Ojiostoh, Klionda fell asleep . . . somehow knowing he would not wake again. Or so he thought.

Longhouses were communal homes, about 60 ft. long by 18 ft. wide with pointed or rounded roofs about 18 ft. high and doors at both ends with a post-and-beam or bent sapling frame. They were covered with slabs of elm bark about 4 ft. wide by 6-8 ft. long. They were divided into compartments for several families with platforms for sleeping. Cozy, central fires warded off the cold of winter.

Indian women used sinew thread, taken from the tendon that runs along a venison backbone to make snowshoes. The sinew was used wet. When it dried, it would never break. Venison - animal meat and skin - was an important resource to these hunter-gatherers and farmers.

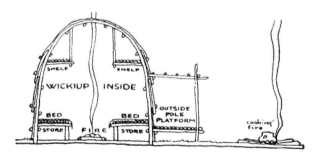

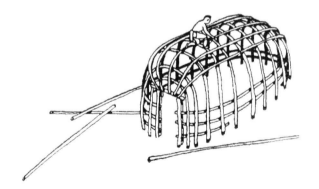

The Great Spirit had watched as the soft, warm wind of the Spring God swept northward bringing softer snow and thawing trees. As Klionda woke to a dark, damp, bleak dawn, he knew the Great Spirit was with him. He stood erect to welcome the new day.

Klionda, the Mohawk had traveled far from home, "living on the trail," like so many other tribesmen hunting in season. In winter, Indians wore moccasins of moose hide lined with rabbit fur, full length fur arm muffs, and long leggings with fringe and designs, to keep the legs warm for wading in snow drifts.

Klionda used a tomahawk to get food and for protection, a Mohawk survival method. The true "tomahawk" was a smooth polished axe-head or "Celt" of stone driven into a hole in a wooden grip that could stop any animal or man.

Groundhogs, like Nawgeentuck, grew enormously fat toward the end of summer, to carry them through the fall season and prepare for their long winter sleep. In spring they were known to dig through snow to reach daylight.

Suddenly, before his eyes, the snow moved and a small hole appeared. Through it peered the small black nose and brown furry head of Nawgeentuck, the groundhog! Klionda's tomahawk struck! The groundhog became the food that saved his life!

Thus, the story of Klionda, the Mohawk Indian and Nawgeentuck, the groundhog who saved his life is still told. Ever since, on the 2nd day of the 2nd moon of the year, Nawgeentuck emerges from his snug lair beneath the snow. Someday, he may again save a life, as he did Klionda's so many years ago.

Groundhogs, which are related to squirrels and prairie dogs, were trapped for their fur, and their meat was considered a delicacy. For protection, their burrows have a main entrance with escape, or "spy-holes" for safety from enemies.

Many centuries after the Indian story of Klionda, other legends of weather seers and prognosticators evolved. These later traveled with settlers to the "New World."

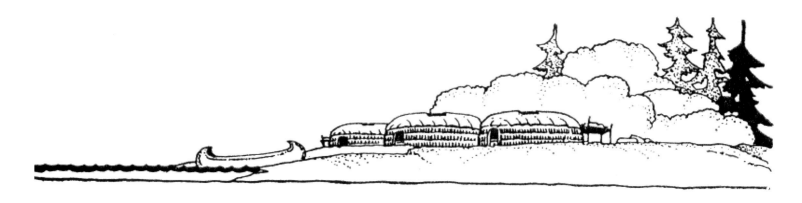

GROUNDHOG SIGHTING

Every now and then, strange things occur in the animal kingdom. For better or worse, quirks of nature make one animal stand out in a crowd more than the others. And that's just what happened with the birth of one very special groundhog.

His beginning was not that unusual. It's just that no one recalled ever having seen a groundhog of such extraordinary colour, or lack of it! And then there were those eyes that saw things in a different light, with the ability to see through shadows with greater insight.

"If you've seen one groundhog, you've seen them all," or so it was thought. All that is officially known for sure, is that this groundhog is a descendant of a distinguished family of marmots that lived in the hamlet of Oliphant, Ontario, a rocky finger of land jutting north between Lake Huron and Georgian Bay of Canada.

Unlike most groundhogs, he knew from the beginning that something made him special. The more he grew, the more he realized just how different he was in appearance from other members of his family. But, there was more to this groundhog than met the eye!

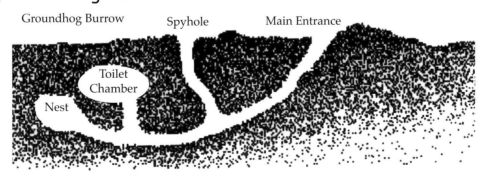

Groundhog Burrow   Spyhole   Main Entrance

Toilet Chamber

Nest

Since most groundhogs lack distinguishing features, it's hardly likely they would stand out in a crowd. But if one is born albino - lacking normal pigmentation and markings, having white fur and pink eyes - its very appearance makes it more likely to get recognition. But, for a groundhog that is thought to spend most of its winter hibernating, what difference could its colour make?

In the dark ages of antiquity, 1956, a secret emissary of three groundhogs shared news of the birth of their fellow groundhog with Mac McKensie, who lived on the shores of Lake Huron. He was in the village of Oliphant anticipating a message of great importance.

Little did he know just how important the message would become.

Most groundhogs are similar in appearance and habitat, living in burrows across all of North America, both in Canada and the United States. Groundhogs are members of the marmot family, which includes such distinguished members as hedgehogs, woodchucks and other stocky, coarse-furred rodents. They have short legs and ears and bushy tails and tend to resemble oversized brownish-grey squirrels or prairie dogs. But, then there are exceptions . . .

Thus, began the life of Willie, the famous albino groundhog born on the Bruce Peninsula of north-central Ontario, Canada. His mystique was further enhanced by the fact that he was born on the 45th parallel, midway between the Equator and the North Pole.

Watch out for Willie! His position on things could be influenced by what he saw.

The three groundhogs named Muldoon, Grundoon and Sand Dune chatted excitedly in Groundhogese, the official language of groundhogs, about this special white groundhog and his extraordinary ability to predict the weather. Mac spread this great news to everyone!

Every year the people of Canada, chilled by the blustery cold of winter, hoped for early spring. Eager to know the extended weather forecast, the nearby town of Wiarton, Ontario adopted this white groundhog as their own and christened him Wiarton Willie.

There was no shadow of doubt that he could predict the weather every February 2nd, which became a day named in his honour.

Groundhogs have both summer and winter burrows, each with a main entrance, separate toilet and nesting chambers. The winter burrows of hibernation are usually deep below the frost line.

Since groundhogs live in open fields and meadows, clearings near forests, and even on rocky slopes, their homes vary according to location.

It so happened that Willie of Wiarton's burrow was in the right place at the right time to have a day named after him. Canadians await his weather prediction when he appears on Williemas Day!

But there's more to the story than its beginning, and more groundhogs of Groundhog Day than one could ever surmise.

From its beginning, the town of Wiarton was as special as its groundhog, Willie. It was a landing stage for natives and voyageurs portaging their canoes and cargo across the narrow part of this peninsula to Lake Huron. Thus, they avoided the more treacherous waters at the tip of the Bruce Peninsula.

Of all the groundhogs that think they can predict the weather, this extraordinary one is not only difficult to see, but whose message is often hard to find. Perhaps it needs an inside-out shadow to find itself . . . albino, of course. How else could a groundhog, known to the world as Willie, make a prediction that casts light on a message, assuming he can see himself when reflected against the snow.

Wiarton sits squarely at the head of Colpoys Bay and was named after Wiarton Place in Maidstone, Kent, the birthplace of the Governor General of Canada during the 1850's. What used to be a small lumbering town is now a thriving community with stores and homes.

It's normal to be somewhat confused with bits of information coming from Groundhog Central in Wiarton about an elusive white, albino, groundhog, named Willie. His story is unique when it comes to weather predicting.

On the other hand, there are bound to be others that refute his prediction, have ones of their own, or even claim to be the first of the weather seers. But Indian folklore may predate any prognosticators of today.

SHADOW CASTING

Willie realized the dilemma of the human world and their uncanny need to know just how long winter would last year after year. His time had come to give them a message. But, with his message came his shadow following close behind.

Who could better resolve the weather problem than a soon-to-be famous prognosticator of Canada, the very distinguished groundhog, Wiarton Willie. The powers of this groundhog were extraordinary. But to understand him, is to understand the importance of his shadow.

Some say he awaits and then repeats the weather prediction of America's Punxsutawney Phil. But, others know better.

The cold winds of winter harbor a legend about another groundhog, named Phil, that predicts the weather in the United States. He has existed for more than one hundred years in the Pennsylvania town of Punxsutawney. Indians named this place, Ponksad-uteney, a town of sandflies.

Punxsutawney Phil was also at the right location at the right time. He lived at Gobbler's Knob, a hilltop overlooking the town. Almost seventy years before the emergence of Willie, Phil gave his first official forecast, February 2nd, 1887.

Before long, other groundhogs were emerging from their burrows to predict the weather around America. Jimmy, a groundhog from Sun Prairie, Wisconsin wanted to be heard, as did Essex Ed from West Orange, New Jersey!

It's worth repeating that Willie took a place of honour after three wise groundhogs named Grundoon, Muldoon, and Sand Dune proclaimed his birth.

He distinguished his life with an uncanny ability to accurately predict the length of winter when he emerged from his lair in search of his shadow. Little did he know it depended on his ability to shadow cast to find himself.

Willie had a better chance of shadow casting at sunrise, than midday when the shadow is its shortest. Shadows vary at different times of the year as well as at different times of day. In winter the sun is lower in the sky, casting longer shadows. But, if he happened to emerge on a cloudy day, he cast no shadow at all!

A spunky groundhog named Harley was predicting the weather from Greensboro, North Carolina. At the same time, Octoraro Orphie was sending his message from Quarryville Pennsylvania. They knew they could outpredict Punxsutawney Phil if someone would listen to them.

Each groundhog assumed a place of honour in its community for forecasting the weather. But, with so many trying to make a prediction, it left the groundhogs in a predicament. If one groundhog stayed out, would the others follow? How did one groundhog know what the others were predicting?

When these groundhogs started feuding, Willie realized he was not alone as a weather seer!

Willie was known to feel like an "Ugly Groundhog" growing up. He knew he had to overcome his appearance, or lack of it. When he discovered his shadow, he was determined to use it to his advantage. If his shadow scared him back in his lair, there would be six more weeks of winter. However, if he was unable to find his grey reflection in the snow, spring would come early! Every year he looked forward to predicting the weather by shadow casting.

Somehow, Willie had to learn to face who and what he was, and the gift he had. But every time he went out on his own, his shadow followed him. In his younger years of prognostication, Willie was unaware of just how important his shadow was. He was soon to realize that it was part of his mystique!

For any groundhog to predict the weather, it takes the chance of being right some of the time, but not necessarily all of the time. Willie is known to have consistently delivered accurate predictions on the remaining course of winter, ninety percent of the time.

The accuracy of Punxsutawney Phil's prognostications is assumed to be high, but how high depends on just how long one has charted his predictions, since he has been around for well over 100 years.

The course of the weather is said to be determined by how a groundhog reacts to its shadow when it emerges from its lair or burrow each February 2nd. If it cannot find its shadow and stays out, there will be an early spring. But . . . if the groundhog sees its shadow and returns to its burrow, that sends a message to the world that winter will last six more weeks.

As he grew, his confidence in predicting grew . . . and with him his shadow *grew*, and *grew* and *grew*. And Groundhog Central of Wiarton took another leap forward heaping piles of snow to make a sculpture of this white critter, whose statue would later be carved in stone. . . white, of course! Was there any other kind of stone to commemorate his being?

Townsfolk were awed by the stately and massive size of the newly emerging Willie. He was on to something, but was not about to let anyone in on his secret except, perhaps, the members of the Lion's Club who believed in him and raised him on a pedestal.

As the sculpture took shape, Willie enjoyed discovering the likeness of himself in stone!

Bluewater Park of Wiarton became the home of the world's largest stone sculpture of a groundhog. Titled "Willie Emerging" it was sculpted by Canadian artist David Robinson from dolomitic limestone, which is indigenous to the Bruce Peninsula.

This groundhog sculpture was commissioned by the Wiarton & District Lions Club of the Town of South Bruce Peninsula to commemorate the 40th anniversary of the Groundhog Festival and Willie's predictions.

Bluewater Park has a Victorian train station, baseball diamond, playground, a boat launch and long dock for fishing, strolling and watching the sunrise.

FOREVER WILLIE

Willie had to live up to his name and understand the role his shadow played in determining the weather! And he knew, above all else, that the forecast had to be as accurate as possible, considering he was a groundhog!

The shadow that he carried around came into view or stayed out of sight dependent on the amount of light that surrounded him! Shadow casting might help him predict the onset of spring, but not necessarily change it!

The people of Canada relied on his prognostication skill! Since Willie could only speak in Groundhogese, it was left to his handler and the Mayor of Wiarton to interpret the annual forecast.

Willie is recognized as the first albino groundhog to thwart the Laws of Nature, by being able to cast a shadow against the white snow. The natural world is filled with cycles . . . highs and lows in temperatures and weather . . . seasonal changes that come when least expected.

Willie has the ability to anticipate weather changes, especially on February 2nd, the astronomical midpoint of winter with six more weeks remaining.

"If Groundhog Day is sunny, and the groundhog sees his shadow, he'll be scared back into his hole for six more weeks of winter."

As Willie aged, he became known as the Enlightened Groundhog. He knew when to emerge from his spyhole, but if he spied his shadow, return quickly to his burrow for six more weeks of winter. Since he was albino, there was a fair chance that his shadow could find him, before he could find himself against the snow.

Some think that his message and Groundhog Day are only for people. But, Willie knows that if he doesn't see his shadow and stays above ground, all the hibernating animals will be pleased with an early spring!

On the other hand, even plants and trees look forward to blooming in spring.

Just as the hibernating animals think they can slumber away winter, the month of January blows off the calendar. With February, everyone waits for February 2nd. And . . . with February 2nd comes the emergence of Willie, in search of his shadow.

He is an established citizen of Wiarton who is known as a groundhog of great integrity . . . a representative that displays the good qualities befitting humankind.

Willie's permanent dwelling is on the front lawn of Wiarton Willy's Motel, at the south end of Wiarton. He enjoys visitors, but gives only one prediction a year.

When Willie's handler went to waken him January 31, 1999 to prepare for the coming events, Willie did not respond. His burrow was silent - very silent. The worst was confirmed. But Willie, in his infinite wisdom, left a message for his last Groundhog Day prediction that February.

Wiarton Willie displayed to the world, an animal that could overcome fears and lack of confidence as he matured. He not only experienced the reality of life, but sent a message around the world for everyone to enjoy.

The search for a new Willie began in earnest! Thus, it gave everyone great pleasure when another albino groundhog was found.

Over the years Willie had relatives stand in for him at other events. When Willie succumbed after preparing his prediction of 1999, a fellow groundhog stood in for him and delivered his message to the Shadow Cabinet.

Thanks to Wee Willie, the legend of Willie will be around forever!

Wee Willie was discovered in Ottawa, the capital of Canada. His home, like that of Willie, was close to the 45th parallel, midway between the Equator and the North Pole. With his white fur and pink eyes, Wee Willie also looked like his famous forefather, Willie!

When he was flown to Wiarton to fulfill his responsibilities as an heir apparent, he was greeted by Willie's handler.

Wee Willie shares similar interests with Willie. When not answering his e-mail, his summers find him holding court for tourists and visitors, basking in the warm Bruce Peninsula, sailing on the waters of nearby Georgian Bay or hiking along Bruce Trail.

Pre- and post- hibernation find him on a snowmobile or following cross-country ski trails. He also spends his time in front of the tube, or TV, watching his hero, Red Green, or reading his favourite magazines, *Canadian Geographic* and *Canadian Living*.

But in summer and fall, Wee Willie must practice his new weather prognostication skills.

Once he became familiar with his surroundings and comfortable with his handler, he was introduced to his new "digs" or burrows. His meals consist of dried pellets, carrots, apples, corn and dandelions.

Wee Willie is often seen sniffing the air, gazing at the sky and listening to the sounds of wind, trees, birds and nature. This helps him better understand the cycles of life and the seasons, as he practices and refines his weather prognostication skills.

In fall, his home is filled with straw, in which he can burrow deeper tunnels of hibernation. When he emerges briefly through his spyhole, there is always food and water for a light meal.

Whatever the season, Wee Willie welcomes visitors to his home.

WILLIEMAS DAY

For every holiday there is a beginning, and this one is no different. It all started with the three groundhogs, Muldoon, Grundoon and Sand Dune that declared the birth of an albino groundhog.

After Willie was adopted by the town of Wiarton in 1956, festivities surrounding his weather prediction started in a meeting room of a motel that became known as Groundhog Central. Phone lines were installed for volunteers to carry Willie's message from Canada to countries of the world.

Wee Willie carries on the traditions of Groundhog Day with youthful exuberance!

Willie's weather predictions are part of the Wiarton Willie Groundhog Festival celebrations. On Williemas eve, the night before his message, there is a Wake-Up Willie party!

Many songs have been written about Willie including, "Wake Up Willie," "The Groundhog's Day," and "Don't Touch My Willie," done in Groundhogese. There is even a song about the sculpture, "Two Ton Willie."

The staff of the Town of South Bruce Peninsula, members of the Chamber of Commerce and the Lion's Club and the public comprise the festival committee.

Wee Willie realized the importance of the legend of Wiarton Willie when he assumed his duties.

Wiarton Willie's new slogan of the 21st century is, "To Serve and Predict." He has become a Neighbourhood Watch member looking after his community. He also serves as an ambassador for the Town of South Bruce Peninsula to the world.

The festivities of Williemas Day begin with a Prediction Pancake Breakfast. This is followed by a Shadow Parade to his burrow. The Shadow Cabinet awaits Wiarton Willie's weather forecast, whose accuracy is revered by other groundhogs and human weather predictors.

The media and visitors eagerly await the yearly prognostication of Wee Willie at his best!

The Wiarton Willie Festival 2000 was voted the Most Popular Event in Ontario! Wee Willie was at the right place at the right time to merit the honour of becoming Wiarton Willie - the one, who like his forefather, has become the leading weather prognosticator of Canada.

There is even a Groundhog Day Menu honouring him and Williemas Day. It includes Groundhog Helper, a tasty one-pot dinner; Willie's Cousin Meatloaf; Six More Weeks of Winter Tortilla Stack; See Your Shadow Soup and delicious Wiarton Willie Cupcakes.

The ancient rituals of Candlemas were replaced by the celebrations of Williemas. Thus, from the simple message on Williemas eve to Mac and Oliphant's residents, has grown the true meaning of winter . . . Have a wonderful Williemas Day!

Wiarton Willie's Official Directory

Wiarton Willie
Bright, White
Out of Sight
Never wrong
Always right
Wiarton, Ontario
Groundhog Capital
of Canada

E-mail address: willie @ bmts.com
Internet Site: www.wiarton-willie.org
Mail: P.O. Box 310, 315 George Street
Wiarton, Ontario
CANADA N0H 2T0

Phil's Official Directory
E-mail address: pcoc@penn.com
Internet site: www.groundhog.org

For Further Reading

ATLAS OF THE NORTH AMERICAN INDIAN, Revised Ed. (Checkmark Books, Imprint of Facts On File, Inc.,NY), 2000.

CARVED IN STONE- The Legend of Willie. Dee Cherrie Ashman (Alea Design & Print, Mayne Island, B.C., Canada), 1996, 2nd. ed.

ENCYCLOPEDIA OF NATIVE AMERICAN TRIBES. Carl Waldman. (Checkmark Books, Imprint of Facts On File, Inc. NY), 1999.

PEOPLE WHO LOVE GROUNDHOGS AND ITS PEOPLE. Elaine Light. (Spirit Publishing Co., Punxsutawney, PA), 1982.

THE HIDDEN SHADOW. Barbara Birenbaum. (Peartree Books, Clearwater, FL), 1987, 1993.

THE STORY OF PUNXSUTAWNEY PHIL. Julia Spencer Moutran, Ph.D. (Literary Publications, Avon, CT.), 1987.

THE UNOFFICIAL GROUNDHOGESE DICTIONARY. Judy C. Freed, Terry A. Fye. (Spirit Publishing Co., Punxsutawney, PA.) ,1994.

Dictionary

Borough - a self-governing incorporated town.

Burrow - a hole or tunnel dug in the ground by a small animal for shelter and protection.

Candlemas Day - ancient name for the midpoint of winter, February 2nd.

Essex Ed - the groundhog of West Orange, New Jersey that predicts the weather.

Gobbler's Knob - site where Punxsutawney Phil makes his annual prediction at Punxsutawney, Pennsylvania.

Groundhog - stocky, coarse-furred rodents having short legs and ears and bushy tails. Also includes woodchucks and hedgehogs.

Groundhog Day - the day of extended winter weather predictions each February 2nd.

Groundhogese - a rare but scholarly language first formulated by veterinarian-linguist Dr. Doolittle in an attempt to communicate with hedge hogs, woodchucks and other lovable rodents. The way in which Wiarton Willie and all legendary groundhogs communicate.

Grundoon - one of the three groundhogs that recognized Willie's extraordinary abilities.

Jimmy - groundhog from Sun Prairie, Wisconsin that thinks he can predict the weather.

Harley - Groundhog of Greensboro, North Carolina that predicts the weather.

Klionda - legendary Mohawk Indian.

Lair - another name for a burrow, used in Canadian folklore.

Marmot - family of animals including groundhogs, hedgehogs and rodents.

Muldoon - one of the three groundhogs that recognized Willie's extraordinary abilities.

Nawgeentuck - legendary groundhog of Canadian Indian folklore.

Octorara Orphie - groundhog of Quarryville, Pennsylvania, that thinks he can predict the weather.

Oliphant - rocky finger of land between Lake Huron and Georgian Bay of Canada.

Prognosticator - one with the ability to foretell the future, a seer, a mystical visionary.

Punxsutawney - official "Groundhog Town" of Pennsylvania; home of the Groundhog, Punxsutawney Phil.

Punxsutawney Phil - the groundhog and weather seer of Pennsylvania and the United States.

Sand Dune - one of the three groundhogs that recognized Willie's extraordinary abilities.

Seer - one with the ability to foretell the future, a visionary.

Wiarton - community of Ontario that is the official "Groundhog Town" of Canada.

Wiarton Willie - the groundhog known as the official weather seer of Canada.

Wee Willie - the groundhog that replaced Willie in the year 2000.

Words in Queen's English - colour, favourite, honour.

Acknowledgments:

Acknowledgment to the Town of South Bruce Peninsula, Wiarton, Ontario, Canada for granting permission to use the name of "Willie" and "Willie of Wiarton." Their assistance in providing research was invaluable. Pictures provided by the Town of South Bruce Peninsula appear on the following pages: Front and back covers, iii, 10, 15,17-21, 23.

Further research provided by the Canadian Wildlife Service. This book has been enhanced with pictures adapted from THE BOOK OF INDIANS by Platt & Mink Company on the following pages: 2-7.

Special thanks to author Dee Cherrie Ashman, for granting permission to reference her book, CARVED IN STONE.

About the Author

Barbara Birenbaum is an avid naturalist who was always surrounded by uncanny pets. She gives character to the animals in stories, nurturing the unique nature of their being. She enjoys delving into the diversity of life across North America, both in people and nature, their homes and habitats, even nuances of language be it English or squeaks and squeals of a groundhog in Groundhogese. Barbara finds beauty in what brings people and nature together, enriching the lives of humans. THE HIDDEN SHADOW was her first book about groundhogs. She continues to write about other groundhogs and their interesting stories.

Most recently, Barbara was a literary representative for the State of Florida, Division of Cultural Affairs, and served two years as a poet of Pinellas County, Florida, Arts in Education. She was an author honoree at the Adler Literary Conference, the Statue of Liberty and United States Groundhog Centennials. THE OLYMPIC GLOW was in the Curriculum Guide to the Atlanta Olympics. AMAZING BALD EAGLET is the first in a series of A Story Within A Story.©

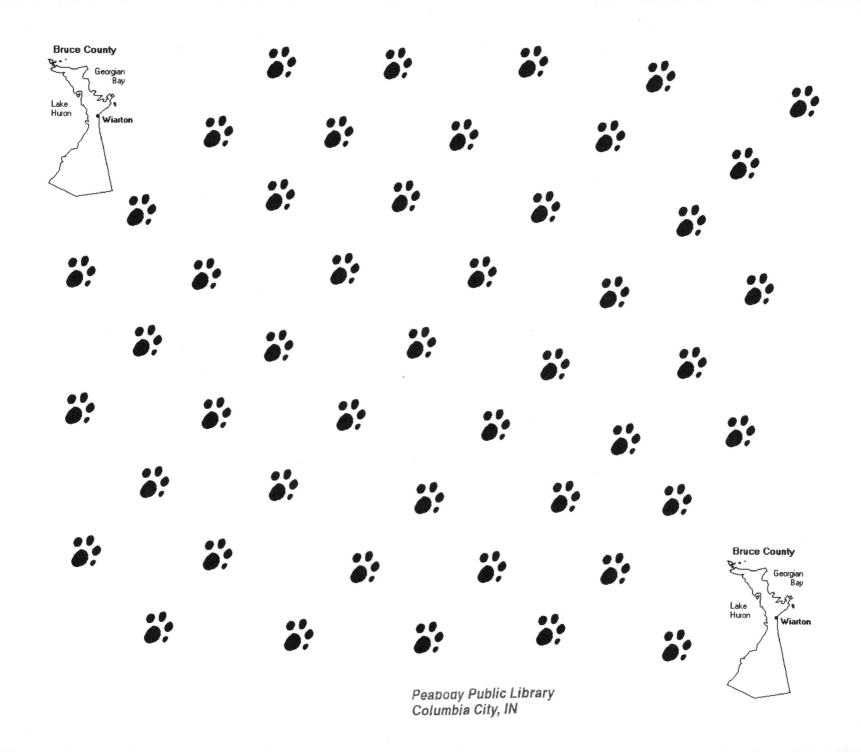